EPA's Response to
External Peer Review and Public Comments of
"Preliminary Steps Towards Integrating Climate and Land Use: the Development of Land-use
Scenarios Consistent with Climate Change Emissions Storylines"[1]
(EPA/600/R-08/076A)

---

[1] Final product title, "Land-Use Scenarios: National-Scale Housing-Density Scenarios Consistent with Climate Change Storylines"

EPA Responses to Peer Reviewers' Comments

(1)   Does the report address its stated goals and if not, what are your recommendations for improving the report?

Reviewer	Reviewer Comments	EPA Response
Daniel Brown	The report could be a little bit clearer in its body about its specific objectives. I find it somewhat unusual that there is information about the goals and content of the report in the executive summary that I don't see in spelled out in the introduction. The summary should summarize the content, meaning that the same content should be available only in more detail in the body. As the body of the report reads now, it is a bit abrupt in its movement from general statements about climate change and land-use change to specifics about what was done in the project, with little in the way of content that would motivate or frame the rest of the document. So, one suggestion would be to include in the introduction to the document a clearer statement of the objectives of the project and of this, apparently interim, report. This statement could include an indication of why this is a good stage at which to produce the report and what the next stages will be. Of course, this later question is spelled out in general terms in the section on "Options for Future Study," but one wonders whether there is already some work underway along any of the lines mentioned.	The introduction was revised to reflect comments about goals and stage of project.
Daniel Brown	As for achieving the overall goals of the project, one question I have is whether the computer code and data sets that are referenced in this document are publicly available and now in an easier-to-use format. Clearly quite a lot of work went into the completing the project and, as the goal is to "enable us, our partners, and our clients to conduct assessments of both climate and land use change effects," important steps in achieving the goals are (a) making this process simple to implement so that various alternative scenarios could be explored and (b) distributing the tools that are produced by the project to a wide range of potential users. A number of tools, data sets, and conversion processes are outlined, but nowhere is a URL specified for accessing these tools. As a report on methodology, distributing these is critical to achieving the stated goals.	A GIS-based tool was developed based on this study and is currently in review. This tool is mentioned in the Preface.
Steven Manson	The report meets its chief goal of providing a model for characterizing and assessing the changes in land use in the United States into the future, as measured by housing density and impervious surface cover. This research is especially valuable in how it downscales the widely accepted Intergovernmental Panel on Climate Change (IPCC) Special Report on Emissions Scenarios (SRES). The social, economic, and demographic storylines that drive SRES are tied to specific processes at fine scales, such as migration to the county and imperviousness/housing density down to the hectare. There are areas where the report could provide additional details, and there are others where the model could be	No response necessary

Reviewer	Reviewer Comments	EPA Response
	extended in the course of future research.	
Dawn Parker	I'm basing the stated goals on these outlined in the charge:	No response necessary
	The Global Change Research Program (GCRP), within EPA's Office of Research and Development, focuses on assessing how potential changes in climate and land use may affect water quality, air quality, aquatic ecosystems, and human health in the United States. The GCRP has completed an internal EPA report describing the methodology used to develop future land-use scenarios for the United States by decade to the year 2100.	
	and on the "Preface" text from page vii:	
	…The report describes the methodology used to develop and modify the models that constitute the EPA Integrated Climate and Land Use Scenarios (ICLUS). The scenarios and maps resulting from this effort are intended to be used as benchmarks of possible land use futures that are consistent with socioeconomic storylines used in the climate change science community. The two-way feedbacks that exist between climate and land use are not yet fully understood and have consequences for air quality, human health, water quality, and ecosystems. In this report we describe the first steps towards characterizing and assessing the effects of these feedbacks and interactions by developing housing density and impervious surface cover scenarios. These outputs facilitate future integrated assessments of climate and land-use changes that make consistent assumptions about socioeconomic and emissions futures. EPA's intention is to use the results of this first phase of modeling to inform and facilitate investigation of a broader set of impacts scenarios and potential vulnerabilities in areas such as water quality, air quality, human health, and ecosystems. More specifically, this research will enable more sophisticated model runs that will evaluate the effects of projected climate changes on demographic and land use patterns and the results of these changes on endpoints of concern.	
	I would like to make a careful distinction between 1) whether the report addresses its stated communication goals and 2) whether the model developed by the authors meets the goals set out by the EPA and the authors.	
	With a few exceptions described under question 2, the report meets it stated goal to "describe the methodology used to develop and modify the models that constitute the EPA Integrated Climate and Land Use Scenarios (ICLUS)."	

Reviewer	Reviewer Comments	EPA Response
Dawn Parker	The model presented is, as the authors state, a first step. The team is to be commended for developing an approach, based on existing and available data, that attempts to project migration and residential land-use change for the entire US. However, for reasons that are described in greater detail below, it is my assessment that the model that the have developed is not yet ready to be used to project land-use changes that can then serve as inputs into other environmental assessment models for the purpose of policy analysis. My main reasons for this conclusion are: • The report does not review, make reference to, or make comparisons to other regional and national land-use change models that were developed elsewhere with similar goals.	Theobald (2001, 2003, 2005) compared SERGoM to other modeling efforts, including a couple suggested by the reviewer. The general difference is that most models are based on assumptions that require very spatially detailed data such as those at the parcel level (e.g., specific land use type and zoning). The more general models that have been developed for countrywide scale by Europeans are more general. None of the models developed in the US suggested by the reviewer have been developed for the entire US -- they are too data intensive... that is why SERGoM is unique. Also, some of the work and citations post-dates the beginning of this project. See report for specific changes and citations.
Dawn Parker	• No estimates of the error and uncertainty of the integrated projections (based on the coupling of three models and on many assumptions) are provided.	Added text to introduction about how this study is intended to explore scenarios, and that uncertainty with any of the outcomes is very high.
Dawn Parker	• No model validation has been conducted to compare the projections of the ICLUS model to real-world land-use change data. At a minimum, in-sample model validation should have been conducted. It is important for policy makers to have information on how well a model designed specifically to produce realistic temporal and spatial change projections performs against real-world data, so that users can assess the level of confidence that they should have in model predictions. Validation also provides important information on next steps for model modification and improvement. (Verburg et al. 2006).	We agree that some type of validation is important. We provided additional discussion of validation in the text. We also added a recommendation that forecasted housing density patterns should be compared to more local and specific models.

Reviewer	Reviewer Comments	EPA Response
Dawn Parker	I am concerned that the coupled models are over fitted and contain too few explicit representations of land-use change processes and the drivers of land-use change. A model that contains few structural elements and is very closely calibrated to a particular place and time is unlikely to perform well outside of the range of calibration data (Verburg et al. 2006).	All models face this criticism -- and it comes back to understanding the assumptions of the model. Again, these are forecasts that reflect specific assumptions that are described in the SRES scenarios. And, other reviewers recognize that this may be a necessary tradeoff. We also added Appendix F, which lists the main assumptions of the models.
David Skole	Yes, but not as well as one would have liked. Indeed, the goals of the project are never made explicit. There is some indication from the Introduction on page 1 lines 14-17 and lines 24-28. The impression is left to the reader that the modeling project will lay a foundation for integrated assessment of the complex relationships between land use change and climate change: "The motivation for the EPA-ICLUS project was derived from the recognition of the complex relationships between land use change and climate change impacts and the absence of an internally consistent set of land use scenarios that could be used to assess climate change effects." This insight into complexity and integrated assessment is never achieved. The report suggests there will be a way to assess feedbacks from climate on land use change and this insight is never achieved in the report. The report should state very clearly that its main intention is to model one form of land use change (housing density and impervious surface) to estimate its effect on greenhouse gas emissions.	Revised Executive Summary and Introduction to make goals clear.
David Skole	It is not possible from this report and the methods it used to even make a statement on land use affects on climate since the study does not include an explicit method for linking resulting land use changes with surface conditions, sensible and latent heat flux or other similar biophysical parameters. It is probably not readily possible to link the results of this study to greenhouse gas emissions since there are many non-modeled sources. For instance the land use effect on carbon stocks (e.g. forest loss) and on gas exchange (e.g. nitrous oxide in agriculture) are not considered. Hence the reports needs to make it very clear what it can and cannot achieve, starting with an clear statement of goals – and not mis-represent this approach as "complex" or "integrated".	Added this clarification to Introduction.
David Skole	A very clear example of the lack of integration is shown in the migration gravity model development, in which historical average climate conditions are used. The report suggests a literature that shows strong relationships between migration locations and climate, yet, rather surprisingly, the model uses past conditions – no attempt is to incorporate	Added text to the introduction clarifying that this report describes the first phase of the project, and that such integration is a likely future

Reviewer	Reviewer Comments	EPA Response
	new climate parameters.	step.
David Skole	This reviewer's suggestion is to re-craft the entire Introduction with a very clear overview of Goals and Objectives. Be very clear that the rather simplified, if not simple, method to spatialize demographic trends is merely a first attempt to recognize the geographical variations in potential land use changes derived from population density location.	Clarified goals and objectives in Introduction.
David Skole	There is confusion between housing density and the cited work by Lui et al (2003). Lui's work, which I have many problems with anyway, focuses on households not housing density. Their claim is that the number of households is a better predictor of land use change and other environmental impacts than population alone. The household metric is not necessarily coupled to population density, and they have used this concept extensively to model a far ranging array of impacts, including such things as divorce which tends to make two households out of one and has no bearing on population dynamics. The EPA analysis includes a variation in household size but only as a function of fertility, which is reasonable but not the same concept as Lui et al. (2003). I suggest the authors steer clear of associating their approach to that of Lui et al (2003) and focus, as they have, on trends in housing density derived from population characteristics.	The Liu, et al. reference was removed.
David Skole	There are a number of land use change modeling efforts underway and many different approaches and methods. Usually the method used is a function of the goals of the analysis. It is not at all clear that the methods selected are related to any of the goals, what ever they are. Since the methods selected for this study have some obvious limitations, it is important that the precise logic for selection of the methods is clearly traced to the goals. The authors should, again, write the goals clearly up front – and perhaps early in the text also include expected outcomes.	The Introduction was revised to reflect goals. Other reviewers commented on methods as appropriate.
David Skole	Lastly the same can be said for the rationale to select the SRES so-called storylines as the basis for scenario analysis. Especially because they had to be changed so much for the downscaling, it is not at all clear that this was the best way to select scenarios. Again, an improved description of goals and objectives would be warranted.	The Introduction was revised to state goals more clearly and describe the rationale for selecting and modifying the SRES storylines.
David Skole	The bottom line for this reviewer is that the approach taken may not be suitable for all climate impacts or emissions modeling and as such would seem flawed and inaccurate in the context of many requirements that I can think of. The approach appears to take a population growth model,	The goals of this study were clarified in the Introduction. Regarding scale, the land use change model operates at a 1

Reviewer	Reviewer Comments	EPA Response
	modified by migration at a county scale and then spreads these people over the landscape using some simple spatial allocation model mostly derived from allocation weights based on urban travel distance. It is hard to rationalize that this is a good approach – and that the 1 ha spatialization appears to be much finer resolution than can actually be modeled. To be honest the first order impression I had is that it's a simple, unrealistic depiction of land use change that lacks any theory or processes. Yet, such an approach may be perfectly reasonable for a simple county-based assessment of settlement patterns and density over time in order to estimate, for example, transport emissions or household energy distribution and consumption and associated carbon dioxide emissions. It may be practically ineffective for estimating nitrous oxide emissions from agriculture (without knowledge of fertilizer application rates) or the effect of forest conversion for bio-fuels or intensive forest management on carbon dioxide emissions, or the effect of climate on Net Primary Productivity. It is hard to form an opinion on approach without knowing exactly what the goals, objectives, and expected outcomes are thought to be.	ha resoultion -- but we are clear that any analysis of the model should be aggregated up to at least 1 km2 (which is why we did this for the impervious surface analysis). The 1 ha resolution allows for major land cover and transportation structure to be better modeled.

(2)   Is the methodology explained in sufficient detail? What additional details or information should be added to the report?

Reviewer	Reviewer Comments	EPA Response
Daniel Brown	By and large, I think the methods are well described. I admit to some confusion in the description of the SERGoM processes, especially in section 4.3 on adapting SRES scenarios into SERGoM. It appears to me that the modifications to the model outlined in that section are not depicted in Figure 4-1. If that interpretation is correct, I think it's an important oversight and should be corrected. I think the modifications on changes in household size and urban form are important innovations in this project and that their implementation within the context of the SERGoM approach should be made absolutely clear. As it is now, section 4.3 talks about a new allocation weight to reflect different scenarios based on travel times, but it it's not clear how it combines with allocation weights discussed earlier.	Good point, added clarifying sentences in section 4.3. Figure 4-1 conveys the overall model structure -- there are a number of details left out of the flowchart, but that's the balance between a general, overall depiction of a model and the technical details. More boxes and arrows could be added to the figure, but it would obfuscate the overall operations of the model.
Steven Manson	Overall the level of detail is adequate, although there are specific instances noted below where more detail would help in interpreting the model. These relate to the gravity model, apportioning PUMA data, and migration modeling (see comments under Question 3, 5). There is also room for more description of impervious surface modeling and importance of compactness in urban areas (see comments for Question 6)	The IS and compactness discussions have been edited to add more detail. The gravity model and PUMA apportionment discussions were also improved.
Dawn Parker	The methodology is explained in detail. The one point that is not clear is the calibration and role of the housing density and impervious surface cover model described in Appendix C. Was this model developed using modeled housing densities, rather than real-world densities? Did a statistical model of the relationship between real-world housing density and impervious surface feed into the model at some level? Were any of the land cover layers used for model calibration classified based on impervious surface, or were urbanized land uses derived in some other way? Is the evaluation of the model designed to validate how well the residential housing model projects changes in housing density, or how well the model projects changes in impervious surface?	Appendix C was revised to include more detail and clarification for impervious surface.
Dawn Parker	It would also be helpful to have a section that summarizes the many assumptions made in each of the model components.	We added tables summarizing major inputs and assumptions to Appendix F, with references to these tables in the text.
David Skole	The methods were sufficiently explained for this reviewer. I comment on the actual sufficiency of the methods selected in another response. There are two important missing elements that require further elaboration. The first should be a detailed table of all the input datasets and a clear description of them.	We added tables summarizing major inputs and assumptions to Appendix F, with references to these tables in the text.

Reviewer	Reviewer Comments	EPA Response
David Skole	The second should be an explicit discussion of accuracy and validation. The absence of any kind of validation exercise makes this reviewer skeptical of the methodology. There are some very elegant looking approaches with simple implementations (e.g. the gravity model) that have: 1) no clear elaboration in literature, and 2) no validation from historical data, or other suitable validation dataset. The only approximate validation is for five state population estimates, which by review of Figures 3-4 to 3-8 appear to be very poor fits, with the EPA model consistently under estimating the state models. The text dismisses this rather simply. The spatialization model seems to be run on blind faith. This report must make every effort to provide a mapped validation for a location or region.	Regarding the spatialization model, please see responses to Dawn Parker's comments in Question 1. Regarding the demographic model, we provide several references that discuss the widespread use of gravity models for spatial interaction studies. Validating the future projections could only be done against other sets of projections, as sufficient data were not available to run the model for an historical period. Due to the uncertainty associated with any projection effort, we chose to explore multiple possible scenarios.
David Skole	The impervious surface calculation is one parameterization where there is an attempt to provide a validation, but the text on page 39 lines 10-20 is hard to understand, even though there is more description in Appendix C. (The reference to Theobald et al in press is useless). For instance the text beginning on page 39 line 12 is confusing: "A brief comparison of our modeled IS to existing fine-grained (from high-resolution photography) validation datasets resulted in an R2=0.69 (Elvidge et al. 2004) and R2=0.69 and R2=0.96 for Frederick County, Maryland and Atlanta, Georgia (Exum et al. 2005)." For one, Elvidge et al use satellite imagery, and it is not clear how the spatial resolution differences between Elvidge et al and this report matter. I imagine, although cannot tell, that the comparison is done with non spatial data.	Thanks, these comments were helpful in editing this section. We revised the text to clarify the language, and updated the citation to Theobald et al. 2009.
David Skole	Lastly, related to Question 1, what role does impervious surface play in emissions or climate analysis. I can imagine it could – but its not clear from this report how the EPA intends to make the connection.	Although there are a variety of ways that impervious surface (IS) plays a role in emissions or climate, in this document we pursued only the use of IS as a general indicator – not specifically tied to possible changes in carbon cycling, emissions, or heat island effects. We've addressed this in general, e.g. in Section 5.4: Groisman et al (2005) suggest that one potential impact of climate change is an increase in the intensity of individual storm events. Since these

Reviewer	Reviewer Comments	EPA Response
		events are responsible for the majority of impacts to water quality from stormwater runoff, examining the possible extent of impervious surfaces become even more important given the anticipated impacts of climate change.
David Skole	There are some other poorly described section that could be better elaborated. For instance how is the modeled output from this study matched up against the MRLC dataset to derived changes in land cover types, and what happens when there are in consistencies between them.	We added more detail here about the resolution and methods, but it is a simple overlay operation that involves two different data layers.

(3) **Given the goals of this study, comment on the technical merit of the modeling approaches used, as compared with other available approaches. Please comment on strengths and weaknesses of the modeling approaches used.**

Reviewer	Reviewer Comments	EPA Response
Daniel Brown	This is a very important question. While the interactions of land use change and climate change on ecosystems and human societies are important, and there remain a number of open questions to be explored regarding these interactions, the choice of modeling approach here clearly directs this line of research towards answering a particular subset of these questions. While there are clearly a number of simplifying assumptions contained within this analysis, I view this approach less as a modeling exercise and more as a data assimilation and projection exercise. What *is* being modeled is demographic change, though the project takes those as projections given from the census bureau. Beyond that, conversions of demographic projections to land use and land cover impacts are based largely on empirical regularities and stated assumptions. I describe the process in this way to distinguish it from process-oriented models. A clear advantage of the approach taken here, as discussed in the section on SERGoM, is the ability to generate bounded and comparable estimates on a national scale. The assumptions that go into the different scenarios are reasonably clear. The authors have made a case for how well these assumptions represent the SRES scenarios and, while I suppose reasonable people might disagree on these arguments, there is a reasonably high level of clarity on what the assumptions are. If there were a computer interface available for manipulating the assumptions and evaluating the outcomes in real time, it might be more useful for exploratory purposes. No where are the computer resources required produce a scenario identified, but these may be limiting on the utility of such an approach. This is a reasonable approach when the goal is to assess land-use and climate-change interactions in the sense of joint effects for impact assessment. This seems to be to approach being taken here. The approach could conceivable be used to evaluate the relative independent impacts of plausible future land-use changes and plausible future climate changes on a system of interest, as well as their joint effects.	Thank you for these valuable comments. The availability of the GIS tool is now discussed in the Preface and Section 5.4.
Daniel Brown	The most obvious limitation of the approach is its reliance on past experience and data to parameterize future dynamics and outcomes. This assumption of stationarity is very limiting when it comes to land use processes. The authors acknowledge the difficulties of projecting the economic aspects of land use (e.g., due to changes in credit availability, fuel prices, job markets, trade, etc) and use that as an argument for focusing on the demographic drivers. This is a reasonable argument, but it doesn't make the possibility of huge disruptions in past dynamics into the future as a result of changes in these broader economic conditions go away. The fact remains that the approach involves projection of past dynamics into the future, assuming that the future will look much like the past. The manipulation of parameters to match the SRES scenarios is a	These are useful comments, and we added some of these points to our caveats.

Reviewer	Reviewer Comments	EPA Response
	great start towards imagining different futures. However, even with this important activity going on in this project, there are a number of processes or relationships (for example, intercounty migration patterns, association between housing density and imperviousness) that are assumed to be unchanged into the future. It's difficult to avoid such assumptions with this data-driven approach – unfortunately, we just can't get data about the future. Nonetheless, the authors have made a great start towards tweaking a data driven model to represent alternative scenarios.	
Daniel Brown	There are other important interactions, including those between land use and climate, that this approach is not particularly well suited to address. Those are partially acknowledged in the "Options for Future Work" section and involve impacts of climate on land-use change and impacts of land-use on climate change.	We have made edits to both the Introduction and Options for Future Work about the limitations of this approach.
Daniel Brown	The examples mentioned describe how sea level rise or changes in amenity values associated with climate could cause changes in migration patterns and other land-use changes that are not included in the demographic scenarios driving the land-use scenarios. I'm not sure I see a straightforward path to evaluating this scenario with the model as currently structured. Because the model is so closely parameterized with prior observations (e.g., to set the county-county migration flows), incorporating a process that hasn't yet been encountered on a large scale, like coastal inundation, would be difficult.	Thank you for the comment. The authors agree that incorporation of these processes for the purpose of predicting demographic patterns in out-years would be very difficult. Rather, we might use the information developed by ICLUS to help gauge the extent of the problem from the standpoint of how that land is being used. In the case of coastal inundation, if we overlay sea level rise maps in 2050 over SERGoM outputs, how many people will have to live somewhere else? This model will not be able to (nor was it intended to) predict where those people will go instead and when.
Daniel Brown	An alternative direction not mentioned is the possible effects of land-use change on climate. For example, urban heat islands and other large scale land alterations on latent and sensible heat budgets can create significant forcings on climate. In order to evaluate these effects, the land-surface model would presumably need to be linked dynamically to the climate model, so that updated land-surfaces are fed to the climate model at each step. If there is no effect of climate on land-use, then the land-surface series already created could serve this purpose (with more variables generated). If there is climate effects on land use (e.g., through flooding, drought, changes in crop productivity or other effects) then it would be	Examining the effects of land-use change on climate was not an explicit goal of this project, but this is an interesting comment to consider in future studies.

Reviewer	Reviewer Comments	EPA Response
	more complicated.	
Daniel Brown	Also, are there conceivable futures in which large swings in land use that could result in significantly more or less sequestration of carbon in the landscapes? This can't really be evaluated, but might be important, especially if there are policies aimed at climate mitigation are implemented specifically for this purpose.	Examining the effects of land-use change on carbon sequestration was not an explicit goal of this project, but this is an interesting comment to consider in future studies.
Daniel Brown	Other interactions within the land-use system are also important. The positive feedback that causes larger places to grow more rapidly (which Paul Krugman recently won the Nobel Prize in economics for formally describing) is represented in the demographic model (perhaps too well). However, the model doesn't account for changes in industrial and commercial activity associated with these changes and how they might result in different kinds of new attractions in a place. The urban form manipulations in SERGoM could conceivably be used to approximate the observed negative feedback within exurban areas, where nearby development decreases the likelihood of development, through use of varying densities, but these processes are not represented explicitly as far as I can tell.	This is an interesting comment and an area for potential model improvement in the future.
Daniel Brown	Another aspect of the model that is limiting is its deterministic nature, i.e., it produces only one outcome based on the number of estimated migrants between counties and the most suitable locations within counties. This assumes both a high level of certainty that these factors are well modeled and that the people moving and locating have good information and behave uniformly rationally. Variation in outcomes is not admitted to the model, except through the scenarios. In fact, there is quite a bit of both variability and uncertainty within the context of any given scenario that is not represented at all. The outputs of the scenarios, therefore, give the users no information about likelihood or probability or variance of outcomes. Adding stochastic variation to the models would go some way towards providing some of this information.	We created the scenarios to look at different possible outcomes, and acknowledge that the outputs represent only a small range of the infinite potential outcomes. We will explore possibilities of adding stochastic variation in future improvements. The Introductions and Options for Future Study sections were revised to express this.
Daniel Brown	Along these lines, there a few mentions throughout to the "likely" outcomes under land-use change (see pgs. x, 3, 39). I think this word should be assiduously avoided in describing the outcomes from the model and the project. All the authors can say is what is plausible if we accept the assumptions.	Replaced most occurrences of "likely" with some form of "plausible," "possible," or "might," depending on the context. Some are left unchanged where appropriate.
Steven Manson	*Overall.* The model uses appropriate methods, especially in so far as they are standard and well-understood approaches being used in new ways to address outstanding research questions (e.g., downscaling, spatial allocation at fine scales across broad extents). Other commonly used methods that could be used in this situation tend to center on 'black box' approaches such as very complicated systems dynamics models or computational intelligence methods such as artificial neural nets. These approaches could conceivably produce better model fit, but at the expense of transparency and maintaining the assumption of statistical	No response necessary

Reviewer	Reviewer Comments	EPA Response
	stationarity over time.	
Steven Manson	*Internal migration.* The gravity model is an effective approach to migration modeling. Other approaches that could be used, or be used in conjunction with gravity modeling, include spatial statistical estimation or a more process-based model of migration based on survey responses (although some of the literature cited relies on these data). This said, these other approaches would likely run afoul of the limited nature of data available at necessary scales.	No response necessary
Steven Manson	*International migration.* The population model could have a better international migration component that moves beyond the uniform distribution of migrants among counties. This would likely involve county-specific (or perhaps just state-specific) estimates that are driven by past migration patterns or features of counties that appeal specifically to immigrants. In aggregate, the current schema is adequate to the task, but the site-specificity of the model would be better served given the importance of gateway cities and social networks in guiding where international migrants find themselves.	Added discussion of limitations to Section 3.4
Dawn Parker	Again, the authors of the report should be commended for undertaking a first effort at this very challenging modeling task, and also for providing sufficient detail on their modeling methodology so that I am able to make detailed comments and criticisms.	No response necessary
Dawn Parker	In a report such as this one, I would expect to see a brief review of other related models, along with a specific discussion of how their model compares to other approaches. Several quite sophisticated national and regional level models have been developed in European study areas, and some of them have even been coupled with the IPCC scenarios (Engelen, White, and de Nijs 2003; Verburg, Rounsevell, and Velkamp 2006). It would also be helpful to see comparisons to projections from regional models done in the US (Jantz, Goetz, and Shelley 2003; Landis and Zhang 1998; Waddell 2002). Many different approaches are available to model land-use and land-cover change, and the choice of approach is often constrained by available data and research resources. It is also an open question which approaches will be most effective at regional and national scales and over long time frames. Thus, rather than focus on a detailed comparison between the ICLUS approach and previous approaches, I will comment on specific concerns that I have with the ICLUS approach. Some are due to data constraints. The data constraints represent an important policy issue that I will discuss further in question 5.	Similar to Q1, we have added a short discussion of how SERGoM compares with other modeling efforts, including efforts that have integrated SRES scenarios with land use change modeling.

Reviewer	Reviewer Comments	EPA Response
Dawn Parker	I support the use of the IPCC scenarios. These are well understood by the international community and have been used in other, similar modeling efforts. Certainly they should be seen as a starting point, but they are a reasonable one. They have also been used for very coarse-scale economic integrated assessment models. Have any other scholars attempted to downscale these scenarios for the US?	Several downscaled models that look purely at climate (Univ. of WA and NASA, for example) exist and Columbia U has some downscaling to address economy/GDP for the country as a whole. Urban land use study using downscaled SRES is available from the Journal of Environmental Management. Further investigation of these models is a possibility for future study.
Dawn Parker	I am not a demographer, and so cannot fully assess the gravity model used here. However, I am concerned that the county-to-county approach used here fails to capture the multi-scale dynamics of regional vs. local migration and the land-use change that results. The drivers of inter-urban and intra-urban migration differ (Clark and Van Lierop 1987). Drivers such as regional amenity values, employment opportunities, and life cycle stage can trigger inter-urban migration. Once a household has relocated, preferences, income, and transportation networks will influence where the household locates within an urban area. Location decisions of those migrating within an urban area may also be very different than those in-migrating from another region. Would it be possible using the available data to estimate a two-stage migration model, one for example from MSA to MSA, and the second within MSA?	The migration data used to develop this model included a large proportion of intra-MSA migrations, and such migration were built into the regression. It may be possible to develop a two-stage model, though it was not in the scope of this first study.
Dawn Parker	p. 9 section 3.2: Perhaps it would make more sense to distinguish between "immigrant and non-immigrant populations," rather than by ethnicity. What factors drive patterns of ethnic migration?	The race/ethnicity categories we used were driven by the population and rates of change data. The initial population data was not detailed enough to distinguish in this way, and they fertility and mortality rates do not distinguish between foreign- and native-born.
Dawn Parker	p. 11 23-24: How much confidence can we have that the current trends and distributions of migration will continue? It is a concern that the census migration projections seem unrealistic, since they are a model input.	We added text about uncertainty in this area, since changes driven by policy and economics can easily disrupt patterns and projections.

Reviewer	Reviewer Comments	EPA Response
		Multiple scenarios were considered given the high uncertainty.
Dawn Parker	p. 12 17-18: Are these "R2" actually pair-wise correlation coefficients (r2)? How do your results compare to other gravity models?	By definition, the Pearson coefficient correlation is calculated in a pair-wise fashion.
Dawn Parker	I agree that the stepwise regression techniques are not appropriate for this application. It is important to keep known theoretical and empirical drivers of land-use/cover change (LUCC) in the model. If the goal of the model is an aggregate prediction, colinearity between variables, within reason, will have minor effects of the predictive power of the entire model, especially with a large sample. I expect that the model coefficients would need to be updated over time as more data became available, yet another justification for not omitting known drivers of LUCC. For example, what about employment?	We acknowledge that employment is an important driver of land use change, but chose to omit it due to the difficulty of projecting county employment throughout the U.S. into the future. We chose to focus on more predictable demographic processes. While this does ignore a driver of LUCC, the scenario-based approach is intended to explore a range of possible futures.
Dawn Parker	Modeling growth as a function of previous growth means essentially the model is a reduced-form temporally autoregressive model. Yet, it is not clear that the authors test or correct for temporal autocorrelation. This also means that counties that grew in the past will be projected to continue doing so, and counties that were shrinking will continue to do so. Such highly inductive, pattern-driven models, in my opinion, are unlikely to be adequate to project land-use change over long time scales. This approach also severely limits prospects for sensitivity analysis with respect to, for example, changes in employment or costs of living over time. There is also the question of future resource constraints. Temperature and sunlight explain a lot of recent migration because water has been available and energy prices have been low. Both factors are changing and are likely to continue to change in the future. These changes could reverse current trends towards Western and Southern migration.	We acknowledge that. All models face this criticism -- and it comes back to understanding the assumptions of the model. Again, these are projections that reflect specific assumptions that are described in the SRES scenarios. And, other reviewers recognize that this may be a necessary tradeoff.
Dawn Parker	p. 14, 31-34: Do absolute cost distances between locations really explain migration? Or rather, is there a threshold at which a move from New York to Denver is really not so different than a move from New York to San Francisco? And, wouldn't the distance from New York to Washington have a different influence on decision making than the distance from New York to New Jersey? Again, maybe some of these	Our analysis found that population exerts a stronger pull than distance, so while we did find an inverse relationship between migration and distance, the gravitational pull

Reviewer	Reviewer Comments	EPA Response
	problems could be solved through a two-stage migration model. The travel cost model is very detailed (likely a reflection of the strengths of the team), but it may be too detailed given the generality of the other model components.	of large population centers outweighs relatively small distance in distance when considering multiple potential long distance moves. A two-stage migration model may improve intraregional migration estimates; future work may take this option under consideration.
Dawn Parker	p. 19-24: It would be very helpful to see the model's projections evaluated against some real-world data. Evaluation against other projections is not sufficient, especially given that the methods used to create those other projections were not carefully examined. These other projections were also made for fairly high growth urban areas. It is difficult to know how to evaluate the models' projections. If current trends continue, they might be accurate, but over a 100 year time frame, trends established over a 20 year time frame are not likely to continue. It is a concern that "the ICLUS model is not able to predict population growth due to migration in small rural counties with high natural amenities" (p. 21, 15-16), given that ex-urban development is a major concern.	It was obviously not possible to check the demographic model's behavior against real-world data, given that only other set projections are available for comparison. Tests might be possible if we began the model in the past and ran it through the present for comparison, though sufficient starting population data were not available. Therefore, we decided that a scenario-based approach intended to explore a range of possible futures would provide value despite high uncertainty about the projections. Some text regarding validation of SERGoM was also added.
Dawn Parker	SERGoM model: A strength of this model is that it forecasts housing density, not simply residential location. The extensive non-developable lands layers that the model incorporates are also a strength. Model performance has also been formally validated to some degree (p. 27, 24-27). However, again, the model is highly inductive and potentially over-fitted to the data. Even a statistical model that contains a larger range of drivers of location (for example, (Irwin and Bockstael 2002; Verburg et al. 2002)) might be more robust for out-out-sample model prediction. Clearly such a model would have to be run on a fairly coarse scale, given data limitations. The model appears to take road networks and groundwater availability as given; clearly these will change over time. This model also very much assumes that historical growth patterns will continue, but not does model the drivers of growth (p. 27, 1 8-12; 28-29).	Like nearly all other land use models, there is an important distinction between what the model allows, and how it is actually parameterized and run. SERGoM does allow parameters such as the road network to change over time -- yet there is simply no data available (nationally) to do this. However, the travel time from urban areas does change dynamically as a function of the emergence of new urban areas, something that SERGoM shares with other

Reviewer	Reviewer Comments	EPA Response
		Cellular Automata inspired models (such as Engelen et al. 2007).
Dawn Parker	p. 26, lines 11-20: This method and explanation are not at all clear.	This section was improved.
Dawn Parker	Finally, as the authors point out, some important feedbacks are not implemented in the model, such as traffic congestion and feedback from climate change. These are important needed extensions, however the underlying methodology may evolve.	No response necessary
Dawn Parker	It is difficult to evaluate the model projections. They very much represent current trends. However, land-use planning and zoning is quite different in the NE than in the south and desert SW, and these difference do not appear in model output. Just one example where better data inputs (zoning constraints, for example) might improve model performance.	Added text under Options for Future Study.
David Skole	As mentioned in Question 1 the goals are not as clearly laid out as they should be, so it is not entirely possible to answer this question. The strongest merit of this approach is to provide insight on the future demographic distributions given current structures of the population and settlements with current trends. It is not possible to use these models to make accurate *forecasts* (predictions) because the drivers of land use change are more complex than they are represented here. As mentioned in the response for Question 1 this approach can be useful for some goals: for instance to lay a foundation for estimating transportation mobile source emissions, or household energy demand and location and its associated emissions.	Revised introduction to clarify goals.
David Skole	But the modeling approach is rather simple and lacks processes. There is no opportunity to look at the complex relationship between land use and climate, with climate feedbacks on land use – in spite of some strong overstatements about integrated assessments in the text.	Revised introduction.
David Skole	There is a growing literature on types of land use modeling and it would have been useful for the report. It may be necessary to state what options for methods the team had and why other methods are not in fact used. For instance urban growth dynamics – ergo sprawl – have been modeled in several ways, some of which are more dynamic than this approach. There is a well developed literature from economic geography on location theory and some interesting spatial models based on Ricardo-Von Thunen rent theory. There are also a suite of regression models built around economic growth models such as REMI. These economic growth models incorporate income parameters and other economic factors in addition to demography. Historical studies of urban-suburban growth (sprawl) show it is strongly tied to economic conditions – a rapidly growing economy yields rapid urban development in the outlying areas. These economic projections are thus necessary for making the projections of land use change. There are also a number of spatial association models, which use co-location of built up land with other	Thanks -- please refer to response to Q1. We added additional citations and reviews to compare to some of these models -- but also cite the Theobald 2001; 2003; and 2005 papers which have cited much of the work that is cited in this comment

Reviewer	Reviewer Comments	EPA Response
	factors to operate the spatial allocation rules. This report's spatial allocation is largely driven by a simple weighting function derived from roads-distance.	
David Skole	The strength of the modeling lies in its early attempt to perform a simple spatial map for the entire US. While I think the modeling is simple and probably does not capture most of the necessary dynamics of economics and land use, focusing too strongly on housing density alone, I think there this is an important study. It has great value as a starting point for further modifications and elaborations.	No response necessary
David Skole	One of the most difficult aspects of this study for this reviewer to understand is the argument for using the SRES story lines. The suggestion made in the text is that the SRES was chosen because it is widely accepted. I found this rationale lacking merit in many ways. First, only the basic so-called story lines were used rather than more elaborate data parameters established from the story lines in the full SRES. Moreover, this report only relies on the demographic storylines when the full SRES had other domains. Second, by the time the down scaling exercises were done to get story lines for the US case, they no longer well matched those of the global or regional IPCC SRES. This then begs the question why to use them in the first place.	We have added some text to the introduction about why the SRES storylines were chosen.
David Skole	The weakness of the modeling method is that it cannot capture some of the more important attributes of land use change and land competition that will likely confront the US landscape in the future. As well, as noted earlier, the models cannot readily account for bio-physical processes associated with land use change – water, biogeochemistry, and energy balance.	Discussion of model limitations added to introduction.

(4)   The endpoints of housing density and impervious surface cover were chosen to provide data for further analyses on environmental impacts. What other endpoints may be relevant to calculate to support the goals of this report?

Reviewer	Reviewer Comments	EPA Response
Daniel Brown	This is really kept wide open in the report's stated objectives. The authors want to enable assessments, but they don't specify what kinds. So, the list of possible endpoints is quite long. One could start with other types of land covers. Probably the most important would be tree cover, as it has implications for carbon storage on the landscape. Agriculture might also be important; as noted in the results, a significant amount of the new housing development in these scenarios would come from agriculture. Because the estimates are driven by demographic change only, evaluations of these other land-use sectors would be nearly impossible within the current structure of the model (clearly another weakness that could be named in answer to Question 3). Clearly the loss of farmland to housing can be represented, but not the creation of new farmland to make up for this loss and because of incentives for biofuels, or the abandonment of marginal farmlands, nor the afforestation of large residential lots in the east.	These are good comments; the authors have modified section 5.4 to include some of these suggestions.
Daniel Brown	If there is an interest in linking to climate models, the outcomes would need to be translated into terms that can be used to represent latent and sensible heat fluxes (LAI, surface roughness, NPP). These can also be important in understand hydrological impacts, through integration with eco-hydrological models. The report suggests that it would be possible to calculate changes in vehicle miles traveled (VMT), as a result of changing settlement patterns, which could then go into emissions estimates. The data could be combined with variables that relate to climate sensitivity, like water availability, temperature extremes, air conditioning availability, etc, and used in assessments of human and community vulnerability under alternative climate scenarios.	These are good comments; the authors have modified section 5.4 to include some of these suggestions.
Steven Manson	*Endpoints*. The endpoints of housing density and impervious surface cover are useful endpoints given the goal of the model. There are others that would be helpful in future studies, as described below, such as non-urban land uses like agriculture or a more explicit focus on transportation. This said, the land allocation schema can be used to assess impacts on all land types and it incorporates transportation networks and commute times, which in turn could be used to ascertain transportation-related impacts (e.g., commuting times and pollutant emissions).	These are good comments; the authors have modified section 5.4 to include some of these suggestions.
Steven Manson	*Imperviousness*. A key advantage of imperviousness is that it can be tied to the rapidly expanding literature on linkages between impervious surfaces and a range of environmental impacts. Overall, imperviousness is one useful proxy for environmental impact (complementing the land cover impacts of residential density) and the report authors are clear to note that this is just one step towards a full understanding of land use/climate interactions.	No response necessary

Reviewer	Reviewer Comments	EPA Response
Steven Manson	*Residential density.* The advantages of imperviousness hold for residential density. The chief difficulty faced in any kind of modeling, but especially with future land use and ecosystem services modeling, is trying to incorporate changes in the economic or technological basis for impact estimation. One advantage of the demographic focus of this model is that it can be tied to different economic or technological dynamics, especially as it relates to housing density (e.g., changes in housing technologies) and other aspects of the human system.	No response necessary
Dawn Parker	These two endpoints are very important for water quality analysis. Many other endpoints are also as important, including changes in forest cover, the carbon sequestration profile of converted landscapes, and calculations of vehicle miles traveled and congestion of road networks under different scenarios.	These are good comments; the authors have modified section 5.4 to include some of these suggestions.
David Skole	This has been addressed above as well. Clearly any use of the models to estimate mobile source emissions could be quite valuable.	No response necessary.
David Skole	As well, the modeling approach could take advantage of scenarios and parameters that take account of land competition. For instance, one could estimate a rate of penetration of bio-fuels into the fuel mix and estimate the land area needed – first for grain and then for cellulose – to constrain the modeled built area expansion. This could be a first order estimate of the effect of biofuels on the geographic distribution of land use change. It would have the effect of constraining the spatialization of housing density – perhaps in much of the same way as does the Commercial and Industrial Land Use (see page 26 line 26). To this could be added a transport cost for biofuel – i.e., the production and processing being done in low housing density areas (rural) and the consumption being done in the predicted high density regions (east and west coast urban). It could frame the start of an analysis of the bio-fuel infrastructure requirements, and also the emissions from production to consumption locations.	These are good comments; the authors have modified section 5.4 to include some of these suggestions.
David Skole	Another endpoint related to bio-fuels could be to build a scenario in which new land expansion is a function of biofuel requirements rather than housing. Instead of driving the model with population, use an estimate of biofuel land demand and the SERGoM model, to estimate the spatialization of grain and/or cellulose expansion. A quick estimation of the amount of land needed to meet all our liquid fuel demand using grain alcohol has been attempted. The current land base supporting grain wheat and bean production in the US is approximately 250 M acres. Grains comprise approx half of this, or about 100 M acres. Of this amount, approximately 23% is now devoted to ethanol fuel production – about 23 M acres -- and this amount produces 3% of US fuel. The global average is closer to 5%. Using the global value, we would need to increase ethanol production by 20-fold over current levels to meet 100% fuel needs from grain ethanol. In the US that would mean increasing the acreage from 23 to 400 M acres. This would exceed the total available cropland by 2 fold and would increase the grain	No response necessary

Reviewer	Reviewer Comments	EPA Response
	producing regions by 4-fold by 2100.	

(5) **What model modifications, additional analyses, or additional endpoints would you recommend to include in a future study?**

Reviewer	Reviewer Comments	EPA Response
Daniel Brown	• Depending on computational resources available for this approach, develop an interactive interface that allows users to interact with the scenarios and incorporate stochasticity into the estimation process so that users can see and evaluate the consequences of the range of possible outcomes given uncertainty and variability in the inputs.	The availability of the tool is now discussed in the preface. In the Options for Future Study, we now indicate that adding stochastic variation will be considered as a possible improvement.
Daniel Brown	• Consider ways to move towards including other land use changes, including in the agricultural and forest sectors.	Mentioned in options for future work.
Daniel Brown	• Also, consider representing variability in the impacts residential development both across the density categories and regionally. I would think that the impacts of a given level of imperviousness vary by ecosystem type and that this variability renders simple categorizations like that used here relatively flawed. Consider just reporting percent impervious by watershed, rather than categories of stress level.	Thanks -- we agree that it would be interesting to examine how IS changes as a function of ecosystem -- and have added this as a suggested future analysis. We have used a legend that applies categories of stress level that is based on past literature and we believe that it generally holds up well. Of course the raw %IS are provided in the datasets and so those could be used as well if the categorical legend is not desired.
Daniel Brown	• I think the density categories should be dynamic, but it seems that they probably are not. This may not be important, since the relationship between density and impervious surface is continuous and not based on the categories. However, I think the allocation still is based on the categories.	Allocation of housing units is not based on IS classes, rather IS is an output or function of housing units. This section was clarified in the text.
Daniel Brown	• Run additional scenarios that try to bracket better the high and low impact outcomes (i.e., explore the space for the best and worst outcomes on some measure) to identify desirable and undesirable conditions and the conditions under which they occur.	Mentioned in options for future work.
Daniel Brown	• Explain why change in imperviousness is at such a high rate in the plains under scenario B2. I understand that it's based on a small denominator, but why the increase – is this an artifact of not allowing people to move out from small counties?	We included maps showing absolute IS and relative change in IS due to artifacts caused by small denominators (see Figures 5-25 and 5-26, for example). Those counties are all very small, with populations ranging from a few hundred to

Reviewer	Reviewer Comments	EPA Response
		about 1,000 people. You are correct that this is an artifact of small counties' exemption from the migration model. In general, our approach has some drawbacks when modeling the smallest counties.
Daniel Brown	• Follow up on the suggestion to analyze the effects of alternative scenarios on vehicle miles traveled (VMT) so that the settlement pattern scenarios can be fed back into the emissions estimation process.	Mentioned in options for future work.
Steven Manson	*Endpoints*. Land use/land cover more broadly conceived is probably the most likely candidate for a new endpoint if the model were to be expanded. Given that the model examines changes in residential density as a result of conversion, another promising direction is examining the balance among non-residential uses such as agriculture or forestry. The way in which the scenario results are linked to NLCD is a step in this direction (e.g., the examination of wetland impacts), which leaves room for a complementary, explicit agriculture submodel, for instance.	Mentioned in options for future work.
Steven Manson	A greater focus on transportation (especially linkages among vehicular traffic, infrastructure development, and urban growth) would also be helpful to better specify commuting effects or better illustrate feedbacks between land use development and transportation. The chief difficulty with dealing with transportation/land use linkages is that there are few truly integrated land use/transportation models that can operate at the regional scale in a way that would work with SERGoM. This is an area of future research more broadly in civil engineering and social science.	Mentioned in options for future work.
Steven Manson	*Scenarios*. One area of additional potential explication is further emphasizing that the global scenarios (especially A1/B1) do not necessarily account for the actual 'story line' of the relationship between demographics and economic development, given the complex interactions subsumed in this relationship. This said, the report is careful to examine how the scenarios are open to interpretation (e.g., page 28). Overall, the qualitative interpretation of the scenarios is plausible (page 7).	No response necessary
Steven Manson	*PUMA interpolation*. One potentially useful extension would be to investigate the effect of apportioning PUMA data spatially amongst counties; relatedly, the basis for this apportionment could be more clear (page 13). Allocating population via an areal interpolation mention that accounts for settlement locations or some other secondary variable may be a useful model extension, especially given the attention to using settlement location in deriving the distance matrix. In terms of verification and validation, internal validation of the model may be a helpful approach (e.g., holding back some data from the calibration phase) versus just assessing model fit and sensitivity (Appendix B), but	Thank you for these suggestions. We have updated the text in section 3.5.1 to better describe how PUMAs were aggregated and disaggregated. When migration records for PUMAs were disaggregated among two or more counties, data were disaggregated to counties

Reviewer	Reviewer Comments	EPA Response
	comparison to state estimates is still the most important step of external validation (page 22).	based on total county population. Although the distance matrix takes settlement location into account, population distribution within counties does not affect the demographic projections in any other way. Future work may allow us to test the effect of our chosen method of PUMA disaggregation, or better data (such as IRS records) may allow us to take an alternative approach.
Steven Manson	*Land types*. In future applications, it would be good to conduct sensitivity testing on how the model deals with the balance between commercial/industrial land use vs. infill/brownfield development (page 26). This may have particular relevance for the 50+ population group given their role in reverse migration (e.g., their influence on downtown condominium development). This lack does not call into the model projections given other sources of variability (per Appendix B), but it is an increasingly important factor in the United States, given the graying of the population.	Mentioned in options for future work.
Dawn Parker	The importance of this modeling task cannot be underestimated. Land-use change has been estimated to account for up to around 25% of anthropogenic carbon contributions, and global land-use change models require robust land-use and land-cover change estimates (Parker, Hessl, and Davis 2008). Modelers in other part of the globe, where resources and data are better than we have in the US, are probably 20 years ahead of us in terms of the development of regional and national land-use change models. National level carbon policies for the US are likely to be developed in the near future. Yet, the modeling community is not yet able to provide policy makers with robust, validated national level land-use change models that are based on cutting-edge science. Given that context, the modeling effort described in this report represents a significant and important investment by EPA.	No response necessary
Dawn Parker	I suggest an adaptive, exploratory modeling strategy where several alternative models are developed, and model projections are formally compared using standard verification and validation tools. This model and its future modifications could be a part of that effort. However, the outputs of this model should be compared to real-world data, and especially to projections from other related models on a regional and statewide basis where possible. Ideally an alternative model should be developed that is more structural and process-based (including models that feed back across time and space and more drivers of LUCC). Investments should be made to facilitate sharing of information about	No response necessary.

Reviewer	Reviewer Comments	EPA Response
	models and results, so that all existing relevant LUCC models and examples of LUCC models coupled with water quality, transport, and carbon models can be accessed and compared. There will not be a single, static answer to the question of which modeling tool will best project LUCC into the next century. Again, we need an aggressive national program to support adaptive, scientifically grounded LUCC modeling efforts. I strongly believe that we cannot build effective water quality, air quality, and carbon policies based on sub-adequate land-use and land-cover change models, and given my extensive interactions with other researchers through conferences, expert workshops, and scientific publication, I believe that other LUCC researchers share this view. For instance, the completed LUCC project and the new Global Land Project (http://www.globallandproject.org/), for which I serve on the scientific steering committee, place a high priority on development of land-use and land-cover data. There is a desperate need to improve the quality, quantity, and availability of data inputs for regional and national level land-use change models. Better coordination is also needed between government agencies related to land-use and land-cover data generation, documentation, archiving, and sharing. Many data resources exist that are simply not available to researchers and/or are not available across agencies.	
Dawn Parker	Examples of data limitations for this model: p. 12 3.5.1: The lack of county-to-county migration data is a major concern. The lack of overlap between counties and PUMAs is another concern. Both have caused down-scaling in this study that is potentially problematic. I suggest Monte Carlo simulation (see, for example, (Lewis and Plantinga 2007)) to evaluate the sensitivity of results to down-scaling algorithms. It would also be helpful to have data on household, rather than individual, migration, and model migration and location choices at the household scale. p. 18 19-21: The authors note additional data limitation related to demographic factors.	IRS records provide one potential source of household migration that we may investigate in the future. However, the PUMA-to-county transition is not necessarily as problematic as it sounds. All large population centers involved the grouping of PUMAs (where no error is introduced) rather than the apportionment of PUMAs. This covered over 70% of the population. Admittedly, our methods would have greater uncertainty with smaller counties. We added text elaborating on our methods and acknowledging both of these concerns.
Dawn Parker	In general: Data on housing density are needed at a finer scale than census units to validate this model. Such data are available only sporadically at a national level, and access and costs to data, when they exist, are uneven.	No response necessary
David Skole	The strength of this approach is the use of a spatial allocation model. However, it would be worth exploring additional ways to spatialize rather	These are helpful concerns. We have added some of these

Reviewer	Reviewer Comments	EPA Response
	than simply on population and weighting a distance function. For instance, economic growth is a key factor well known to influence expansion of the built area. Incorporating REMI type models in a spatial context would be an important future modification. Additionally an improved capability to look at land competition and trade-offs would be useful. Lastly, building more feedbacks into the model so that climate affects on land use could be taken into account would be useful.	points into the discussion of future steps. Adding a REMI-type model would be useful, but was not feasible in this round, hence the focus on developing scenarios to explore a range of possible outcomes.
David Skole	I would suggest the team review carefully the modeling work being developed at the Joint Global Change Research Institute at the University of Maryland. Their EPIC model could greatly enhance the agriculture modeling of the EPA effort (NB I have no affiliation at all with the UMd team).	Thanks, this would be useful to explore to incorporate an agricultural land.
David Skole	A diversity of land-change models exists that explain, predict, and project the kind and location of change in land covers and land uses. Below I list a number of references that could be useful in considering different approaches to modeling, some of which would help the team build more process-level capabilities into their approach. A variety of modeling approaches are used to improve our understanding of land change and to encode that understanding for these purposes of projection and prediction. These approaches include stochastic, optimization, supply and demand, dynamic, process-based simulation, cellular automata, agent-based, and a variety of statistical-empirical models. Coupling land-change models with models of biogeochemical, water, and ecological processes faces a number of challenges but could be part of the EPA future efforts. The spatial and temporal scales of land-change models need to be compatible with both the driving processes of land change and process models of environmental systems, and the land change and environmental models must share specific semantic, onotological, and technical specifications in order to allow inter-model communication and coupling. Thus, although there has been much research that contributes to our understanding of land-use and land-cover change, from an observational or empirical basis, there remains a need to develop models of land-use and land-cover changes at spatial scales from local to global, and time scales from short (<5 years) to long (> 50 years), that are compatible with environmental models relevant for the CCSP and other agencies and programs needs.	Thanks, these are useful thoughts and a number of citations to other modeling approaches have been added, including adding an item to future steps.
David Skole	Land change and the reciprocal interactions with environmental and socio-economic systems have direct and indirect impacts on the health and sustainability of society and of ecosystems yet these are poorly developed in the EPA approach. A synthetic understanding of land-change modeling approaches is needed so that these reciprocal relations can be both studied, in the case of explanatory models, and projected through computer-based tools that encode the best scientific understanding and allows the wide-ranging application benefits agency programs to be realized. Importantly, the study will provide guidance to a wide range of science- and application-based model users on the	No response necessary.

Reviewer	Reviewer Comments	EPA Response
	strengths and weakness of the various approaches. Such guidance is not currently widely available.	
David Skole	Another fruitful area of future enhancements would be in coupling land-change models with models or biogeochemical, water, and ecological processes faces a number of challenges. The spatial and temporal scales of land-change models need to be compatible with both the driving processes of land change and process models of environmental systems, and the land change and environmental models must share specific semantic, onotological, and technical specifications in order to allow inter-model communication and coupling.	We have added some of these suggestions to the discussion of future steps. We have also improved the introduction to better describe what this approach is and isn't suitable for.
David Skole	**Addition Material: a brief survey of models:** *Stochastic* Brown, D. G., Pijanowski, B. C. and Duh, J. D. (2000). Modeling the relationships between land use and land cover on private lands in the Upper Midwest, USA. *Journal of Environmental Management* **59**(4): 247-263. Butcher, J. B. (1999). Forecasting future land use for watershed assessment. *Journal of the American Water Resources Association* **35**(3): 555-565. Muller, M. R. and Middleton, J. (1994). A Markov Model of Land-Use Change Dynamics in the Niagara Region, Ontario, Canada. *Landscape Ecology* **9**(2): 151-157. Thornton, P. K. and Jones, P. G. (1998). A conceptual approach to dynamic agricultural land-use modelling. *Agricultural Systems* **57**(4): 505-521. *Optimization* Riebsame, W. E., Meyer, W. B. and Turner, B. L. (1994). Modeling Land-Use and Cover as Part of Global Environmental- Change. *Climatic Change* **28**(1-2): 45-64. *Supply and demand* Waddell, P. (2000). A behavioral simulation model for metropolitan policy analysis and planning: residential location and housing market components of UrbanSim. *Environment and Planning B-Planning & Design* **27**(2): 247-263. *Dynamic, process-based simulation* Landis, J. and Zhang, M. (1998). The second generation of the California urban futures model. Part 1: Model logic and theory. *Environment and Planning B-Planning & Design* **25**(5): 657-666. Landis, J. D. (1994). The California Urban Future Model: a new generation of metropolitan simulation models. *Environment and Planning B-Planning & Design* **21**: 399-421.	Thank you.

Reviewer	Reviewer Comments	EPA Response
	Stephenne, N. and Lambin, E. F. (2001). A dynamic simulation model of land-use changes in Sudano- sahelian countries of Africa (SALU). *Agriculture Ecosystems & Environment* **85**(1-3): 145-161.	

Cellular automata

Clarke, K. C. and Gaydos, L. J. (1998). Loose-coupling a cellular automaton model and GIS: long-term urban growth prediction for San Francisco and Washington/Baltimore. *International Journal of Geographical Information Science* **12**(7): 699-714.

Clarke, K. C., Brass, J. A. and Riggan, P. J. (1994). A Cellular-Automaton Model of Wildfire Propagation and Extinction. *Photogrammetric Engineering and Remote Sensing* **60**(11): 1355-1367.

Jenerette, G. D. and Wu, J. G. (2001). Analysis and simulation of land-use change in the central Arizona-Phoenix region, USA. *Landscape Ecology* **16**(7): 611-626.

Messina, J. P. and Walsh, S. J. (2001). 2.5D Morphogenesis: modeling landuse and landcover dynamics in the Ecuadorian Amazon. *Plant Ecology* **156**(1): 75-88.

van der Veen, A. and Otter, H. S. (2001). Land use changes in regional economic theory. *Environmental Modeling & Assessment* **6**(2): 145-150.

White, R., Engelen, D. and Uljee, I. (1997). The use of contrained cellular automata for high resolution modelling of urban land use dynamics. *Environment and Planning B* **24**(3): 323-343.

White, R., Engelen, D. and Uljee, I. (2000). Modelling land use change with linked cellular automata and socio-economic models: a tool for exploring the impact of climate change on the island of St Lucia. *Spatial Information for Land Use Management*. Hill, M. J. and Aspinall, R. J. Reading, Gordon and Breach: 189-204.

Agent-based

Ligtenberg, A., Bregt, A. K. and van Lammeren, R. (2001). Multi-actor-based land use modelling: spatial planning using agents. *Landscape and Urban Planning* **56**(1-2): 21-33.

Otter, H. S., van der Veen, A. and de Vriend, H. J. (2001). ABLOoM: Location behaviour, spatial patterns, and agent-based modelling. *Jasss-the Journal of Artificial Societies and Social Simulation* **4**(4): U28-U54.

(6)   Please comment on the public comments submitted for this draft report. Specifically, which comments should or should not be addressed in the final draft?

Reviewer	Reviewer Comments	EPA Response
Daniel Brown	I think the statistical methods are fine. Clearly multicollinearity problems need to be dealt with and stepwise processes are a reasonably standard way to deal with them. Clearly missing variables add little to the predictive power of the model (given the contribution of those included), which is the key measure of importance in this case. The use of Classification and Regression Trees (CART) is appropriate in this case. The authors of the report mistakenly refer to the technique as categorical regression trees, but in fact the method (named correctly in the previous sentence) can deal with continuous measures in the form of regression trees. It's true that it produces discrete estimates, but it is an appropriate method for continuous measures that does not, in fact, throw out detail in the data.	CART was corrected in the text.
Daniel Brown	I understand the emphasis on impervious surfaces; though also recognize the importance of other land changes and mitigation activities by developers, farmers and other land users. This point about mitigation also goes to the heterogeneity of the impacts of impervious surfaces and the critique would be mitigated if the authors backed off on the absolute categorization of all impervious levels into levels of ecosystem stress. There is variability in the relationship between housing density and imperviousness and a stochastic modeling approach could be used to introduce that variability. I don't believe that it would have a huge impact at the national level, but it might also address some of this concern.	Thanks, we reworded the text to place less emphasis on the legend classed (e.g., "stressed") and more on the quantitaive value. We also provided a caveat not to interpret the relative designations too strongly, as these are general indicators of condition only. However, we also reiterate that one of the strongest indicators of watershed health, substantiated by numerous studies, is % of impervious surface, which is why this is an important indicator, and why it is important to help interpret what the general numbers mean in a qualitative way for the general public.
Daniel Brown	The suggestion of looking at the effects individual variables separately in the scenarios is a reasonable one, if the goal is to tease out these individual effects. I don't actually get the sense that the goal is to test what is the more important factor, as implied by this critique, but rather to project plausible scenarios. For that goal, the bundled nature of the scenarios presented is reasonable.	We added some clarifying text in Section 2.2.
Daniel Brown	While I agree that evaluations of Smart Growth alternatives would need to be carefully defined before they can be implemented for scenario development, I don't see any implication in the report to the contrary. Nor do I see any conclusions drawn with respect to Smart Growth that could be regarded as at all controversial (as there are none).	No response necessary

Reviewer	Reviewer Comments	EPA Response
Steven Manson	There was one attached comment, from the National Association of Home Builders (NAHB). Overall, the NAHB comments have merit and should be taken into account as they relate to four general issues: 1) the choice of statistical techniques; 2) the emphasis on impervious surface cover; 3) the scenarios used to assess the impact of land development patterns; and 4) references to Smart Growth. a) There is room to modify or better explain the statistical techniques. The caveats that the NAHB raises about stepwise regression are valid but this approach is a common social science method. As with most statistical methods, the analysis and degree of expertise applied to the analysis is usually more important than the potential foibles of the method. Concerns about multicollinearity could be addressed in the data preparation or model specification steps (e.g., via pairwise comparisons) but including the full model specification after removing multicollinear variables would nonetheless be useful. Otherwise, the report could better explain the rationale and process for using CART to derive imperviousness (page 39, Appendix C).	More explanation was added for CART.
Steven Manson	b) The emphasis on imperviousness is an issue in that there exist other aspects of land cover that can be considered, as noted above under question 5. Nonetheless, imperviousness is an important variable and a useful one when tied to residential density.	No response necessary
Steven Manson	c) The scenario-land use linkages could use more explication in the report, but overall, the way the scenarios are employed here are a useful and accepted way of understanding issues we may encounter in the future. Per comments under question 5 above about scenarios, more could be specified under scenario development, but the report is clear in most respects.	No response necessary
Steven Manson	d) The report could be clearer in how it refers to Smart Growth (SG). There is a growing body of empirical research linking SG to a range of impacts. While these impacts tend to be negative in many respects, there are counter examples and areas of ongoing research that should be recognized (e.g., Handy, S. 2005. Smart Growth and the Transportation-Land Use Connection: What Does the Research Tell Us? *International Regional Science Review* 28 (2):146-167.) More broadly, however, it appears that the report is not speaking to the pros/cons of smart growth per se, but instead to the impacts of 'environmental' perspectives towards land use planning. If regional and urban planners believe that compact growth patterns are environmentally sensitive (leaving aside whether they are or not) then they will likely implement policies to produce these patterns. This seems to be the tack adopted by the report (page 51), but it could be more clear on this point.	Language referring to smart growth is clarified so that it is clear we are referring to low impact development with the term.

Reviewer	Reviewer Comments	EPA Response
Dawn Parker	The NAHB comments should be addressed. It is important to note that home builders have some incentive to protect the natural resource base, since the amenity and non-use values within and in the local neighborhood of their developments are captured in the sales prices of their homes. They may provide local public goods through these incentives. However, since they are not able to capture the benefits from the global public good aspects of open space (such as climate regulation), there is still an important role for agencies such as the EPA for protecting open space and the ecosystem functions that it supports.	We have improved our discussion of CART and IS, and changed how we discuss Smart Growth. Please see responses to other comments above.
Dawn Parker	I share their concern regarding the stepwise regression. While my knowledge of categorical regression is limited, their comments are logical from a statistical perspective. I also agree (as stated above) that vehicle miles traveled are important to examine. Their suggestions for alternative scenarios are also a potential next step that deserves consideration. While I don't share their concern regarding the current references to smart growth, the more detailed investigations between smart growth policies and environmental impacts would be of broad interest for future work.	We have improved our discussion of CART. We have added VMT as a possible area for future work.
David Skole	This reviewer received only one public comment, from the National Association of Home Builders. They address the following comments and I have remarks associated with each of them.\n\nChoice of particular statistical techniques: The comments are valid but do not appear to be strong enough to be further addressed in any significant way. As I have commented before, there is a general tendency in the text not to be explicit about the choices made in methods. I think the authors owe the reader an explanation of alternatives and why the methods selected for this study were chosen. Again, the lack of sufficient validation exercises leaves the report open to these criticisms.	We added some discussion of the use of statistical methods in the impervious surface analysis.
David Skole	Emphasis on percent of impervious surface cover: I generally agree with this comment by the NAHB, and have raised that issue above. Unlike the NAHB I can see some linkages between housing density and emissions, but the link to impervious surface is less strong. One could develop an urban heat island model, or perhaps develop a runoff model that would be influenced by storm intensity, but these are a stretch. I must agree with the NAHB that this emphasis on IS needs considerable justification.	We added more discussion about why we chose to look at IS.
David Skole	Scenarios used to assess the impact of land development patterns: I agree with this concern of the NAHB. There is a strong disconnect in logic with the selection of the Story Lines and the prediction of IS. To remedy this, I suggest the authors strengthen the analysis and discussion of outright land use change – i.e., from agriculture or forest to built and then consider the direct emissions issues associated with these changes. Reduce the level of discussion and emphasis on IS. Generally speaking the IS discussions in section 5.3 (page 39) do not logically fit in this analysis.	We added more discussion about why we chose to look at IS. In the Options for Future Work section, we added that future improvements may involve a stronger focus on other land use changes beyond housing density.

Reviewer	Reviewer Comments	EPA Response
David Skole	References to Smart Growth: The comments of the NAHB are baseless and should not be considered by the EPA. Smart Growth is an unfortunate use of terms in the EPA study, and perhaps a different term could be used. I would recommend some references to the work of the Urban Policy Center of the Brookings Institution for references to the urban decentralization problem and a discussion.	Language referring to smart growth is clarified so that it is clear we are referring to low impact development with the term

Additional Reviewer Comments

Reviewer	Reviewer Comments	EPA Response
Daniel Brown	Although the specific goals of the document are not well articulated in the body of the report, the report does suggest (p. 1) that its results will "(1) enable us, our partners, and our clients to conduct assessments of both climate and land use change effects across the United States: (2) provide consistent benchmarks for local and regional land use change studies; and (3) identify areas where climate-land use interactions may exacerbate impacts or create adaptation opportunities." These goals are important and there is clearly a need within the scientific community to bridge the modeling of land-use and climate change, assess their interactions, and evaluate the possibility for interacting impacts. The executive summary (p. x) indicates that "This report describes the modeling methodology for the EPA-ICLUS project and some initial analyses using the outputs." This is more a description of its content than its goals, but it does make clear that the document is a first step, rather than a complete assessment.	We have revised the Introduction and Executive Summary to better describe the study's goals.
Dawn Parker	**References:** Clark, W. A. V., and F. J. Van Lierop. 1987. Residential mobility ans household location modeling. In P. Nijkamp, ed. Handbook of Regional and Urban Economics. Elsevier Science Publishers, Amsterdam Engelen, G., R. White, and A. C. M. de Nijs. 2003. Environment Explorer: a Spatial Policy Support Framework for the Integrated Assessment of Socio-Economic and Environmental Policies in the Netherlands. Integrated Assessment 4:97-105. Irwin, E., and Bockstael. 2002. Interacting agents, spatial externalities, and the evolution of residential land use patterns. Journal of Economic Geography 2:31-54. Jantz, C.A., S. J. Goetz, and M. K. Shelley. 2003. Using the SLEUTH Urban Growth Model to Simulate the Impacts of Future Policy Scenarios on Urban Land Use in the Baltimore-Washington Metropolitan Area. Environment and Planning B 30:251-271. http://scholar.google.com/url?sa=U&q=http://www.whrc.org/resources/Published_literature/pdf/JantzEnvPlanB.03.pdf Landis, J., and M. Zhang. 1998. The second generation of the California Urban Futures Model: Part 1, Model logic and theory. Environment and Planning B: Planning and Design 25:657-666. http://www.pion.co.uk/ep/epb/abstracts/b25/b250657.html Lewis, D., A.J. Plantinga. 2007. Policies for Habitat Fragmentation: Combining Econometrics with GIS-Based Landscape Simulations. Land Economics 83:109-127. Parker, D., A. Hessl, and S.C. Davis. 2008. Complexity, Land-Use Modeling, and the Human Dimension: Fundamental Challenges for Mapping Unknown Outcome Spaces. Geoforum 39:789-804. http://dx.doi.org/10.1016/j.geoforum.2007.05.005	Thank you for these additional references.

Reviewer	Reviewer Comments	EPA Response
Dawn Parker	Verburg, P., K. Kok, R.G. Pontius, A. Veldkamp, A. Angelsen, B. Eickhout, T. Kram, S.J. Walsh, D.C. Parker, K. Clarke, D. Brown, K.P. Overmars, and F. Bousquet. 2006. Modeling land-use and land-cover change. In E. Lambin and H. Geist, eds. Land-use and Land-cover Change: Local Processes, Global Impacts. Springer Berlin Heidelberg, New York Verburg, P., M. Rounsevell, and A. Velkamp. 2006. Scenario-based studies of future land use in Europe. Agriculture, Ecosystems & Environment 14: 1-6. http://dx.doi.org/10.1016/j.agee.2005.11.023 Verburg, P.H., W. Soepboer, A. Veldkamp, R. Limpiada, V. Espaldon, and S.S.A. Mastura. 2002. Modeling the spatial adynamics of regional land use: The Clue-S model. Environmental Management 30:391-405 Waddell P. 2002. UrbanSim: Modeling Urban Development for Land Use, Transportation and Environmental Planning. Journal of the American Planning Association 68:297-314.